MAGIC THE PICKUP

16 Effective Ways to Attract Women,
and Not Just for the Sake of a Kiss

DONALD CAMPBELL

TABLE OF CONTENTS

INTRODUCTION

How is your game when it comes to the fair sex? Are you the straight-up A-game player who can get just about any lady that crosses his path? Or do you run into rejection eleven times out of ten, with the eleventh time being the girl you could not even summon up the courage to walk up to?

"Welcome to the world. You will grow up to be a man, and you will seek the attention and affections of the opposite sex for as long as you stay on this planet". Every man eventually gets this welcome address delivered to him. It is nature itself that dictates that we will seek the affection of ladies to get some form of satisfaction and fulfillment.

It is everywhere around us in the animal world, and we are no exception. Ever since the ancient men walked on this planet, menfolk have always measured themselves by their ability to attract the opposite sex, and hold them spellbound for a set period. The ancient man, fought over available females in very much the same way any other set of animals do. That game has not changed today. Believe it or not, one of the major reasons we have for doing virtually all the things we do is to improve our luck with the opposite sex.

The ways we dress, talk or act as men have some element of "I want to represent a good catch to the ladies out there. So, all men want to be desired, to be fawned about and command the affection of the ladies. It is a mark of ultimate masculinity and pulling power. It has been so since time immemorial. Wars have been fought, battles have been lost, and empires brought down by men struggling to capture the heart of their beloved.

Still, the game remains as ripe and primal as possible. Now, there is no doubt that we all want the ladies or a lady. Everyone is aware of that, but we all cannot have the ladies. Why? Because the ladies too want certain traits in you before they get hooked to you. Notice that I have used "ladies," the plural form. This is because every man out there has a lady that will be his unconditionally, but very few men can have the ladies. Very few men understand the art that gives them the power to sift through multiple sources and pick the lady they want.

This art has been the subject of many books and shows. More books have been written on the ability to attract women than any other topic concerning men. The simple ability to walk up to a girl, and have her eating out of your hands is a rare trait. That is why you look at that your playboy friend with such admiration. It's why you admire his charm and prowess with the ladies. It is why the ladies flock around him in the first place too.

How can you be like him? How can you raise your "ladies" game to great levels? How can you meet a girl and have her preening and laughing along with you in a minute? Importantly, how can you sharpen up your game to get the woman you want into bed *ASAP*?

These are the questions that made me write this book as a guide for all the men outside there struggling to get a look-in. If you ask men who have been successful with multiple women their secret, you will get a whole catalog of answers, some wild and unsupportable. This is simply because most men do not even know the secrets of hooking the girls. No encyclopedia teaches the art, but this book does come close to being one.

To be honest, I was once like you, a greenhorn in the business you may say. A good deal of the info contained in this book are my own trusted and tested principles that I have seen other people emulate and apply to astounding success. Let me tell you today. There is no man out there that cannot snag ladies if he has the right tools and knowledge. A lot of the chapters are short and concise, so you can read, apply the techniques, and zoom out to try them out immediately. In subsequent chapters, I shall show you the tools you need and teach you how to use them to devastating effect and success. Let's hit the road.

CHAPTER ONE

UNDERSTANDING WOMEN

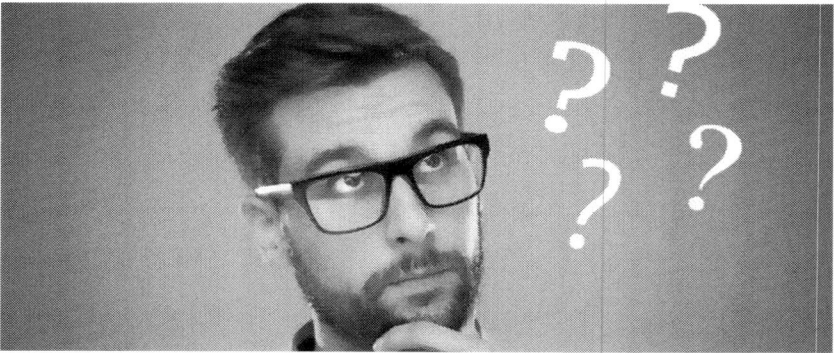

Obviously, I am going to write these words in the belief that you are a fellow man. So, what do men want? Or rather, what do you want in a woman? The answer to this question is the first step in learning how to charm women. For starters, you should be more interested in answering the "what do women want?" question.

It doesn't matter if you want to learn the secrets of one-night stands, learn the ropes for picking up that hot stranger you met at the mall or simply want your ex back, the first commandment is to "know thy target's wants." Then, you offer it to them.

For too long, we have all heard the maxim "women are too complex" too many times, but here's the thing. That saying is both right and wrong at the same time. Granted, no two women are the same. So, in that way, it is hard to apply the same set of rules for different women.

Heck, applying the same set of rules for the same woman in the same circumstances is not guaranteed to work. So, yes, it can be complex getting to know what to do in what circumstances. Yes, women can come across as complex…except if you know the base emotion that guides them.

By understanding the things women want, you may think you can preempt their thoughts and end up right where their minds are guiding them to. But that is so going to get you in the muck or worse, the friend zone.

Instead, play the game women want you to. The goal is to say and do the right things, at the right time to excite the woman in front of you into wanting more of you. Nothing else matters if you cannot do that. If you cannot give a peek at the *mystery* man hiding behind the nice coat or shirt you are putting on, you aren't going to win any new admirers. You don't even need to have any mystery or special thing under the coat, but you sure do need to make a woman feel like you do if you hope to snag her attention quickly in the short-term. Keeping her is another ballgame entirely.

Anyone can play this game successfully. You do not even need to be gorgeous or have a bodybuilder's body (it does advance your case if you do though). You just need to play the game from a vantage point. To do this, you need to learn to flirt. You need to refine your pickup techniques.

Now, how successful you are going to be with girls, depend on some important factors. The major ones are social confirmation, appearance, confidence, conversational skills, charm, and X-factor.

Let us look a bit deeper at each of these.

Social confirmation is the most important of all these factors. In fact, every other factor contributes to your social confirmation. Now, every girl out there likes men just as much as we like them. It is a natural attraction. But yet, not every girl wants to sleep with every man they like. Why? This is because every girl you meet has set standards, and she is not willing to lower them for any man willing to get her to bed. So, they look for you to prove your worth and value. These two things, worth, and value will determine if you get her to bed or not. In fact, they will decide if she replies to your first statement.

You need to prove your desirability to her before you can bed her. You need to show yourself as being worthy of her attention and time. Each line you say while courting her attention will either subtract or add to your worth and value. If after your conversation, you have established enough worth and value, congratulations, you are on your way to her bed. If you have not, you will probably get a firm dismissal, if you are lucky. You hardly get a chance.

So, social confirmation has to happen. She has to feel you and key into your flow. You need to be in sync and hold out sexual tension for her. Confirmation is the game you are playing. Even if she needs good sex as much as you are, you will not be the one giving it to her if you do not prove your worth and value. The first few moments you spend with her lady are her decision period. She seeks for social confirmation that you are a worthy partner. If you pass that test, getting her to bed is pretty easier. If you fail, then trying the second time just got harder.

Your appearance and body language are under your total control. You know they will get assessed for confirmation, and it is a double calamity indeed if you are unable to rig them in your favor. Confidence is perhaps the most important ally you can have in trying to pick up a girl. No matter how important they are, you can survive without any of the other factors, but without confidence, you aren't going to even get a peck on the cheek most likely. Girls can smell low confidence from a mile off. They worsen your blues by presenting a tough front. That worsens your low confidence, and yet another girl slips you by.

When you are confident enough, good conversational skills naturally flow through. The first barrier to a good conversation is a lack of confidence. A girl is more likely to get into you when you are surefootedly leading her in the direction you want. Show signs of self-doubt or allow her to see beyond that cool façade and you are going to get dumped as fast as saying "Jack." Lay on the charm pretty quick too. Forget women alone, even men like people who speak confidently to them and with a touch of class too. Do not be found wanting in this account.

The X-factor is the most elusive thing ever for rookie guys to discover about themselves. Everyone has the X-factor, in different forms, of course. When a girl is trying to meet and know you better, she is all about checking you out to see if you have got your X-factor going for you already. You have it working when walking up to a girl no longer daunts because you are in psychological control of the process. Your X-factor is the playboy in you. You will do well to get it working for you.

The Stages of The Game

I wish somebody had told me or warned me when I twenty that it was I who determined what response I would get from girls. Instead, I always went out on a limb, hands outstretched, searching for signals that would tell me I was being welcomed. Well, it turned out the signals were always pretty conflicting. Is her smile telling me to proceed or a polite way of evading my probing comment? Did she just touch my arm? Does that mean she is flirting with me? Should I move onto the next stage? These questions meant that I was never really in control. Instead, I got played around with because I was relying on too many imprecise signals.

Do not be like my twenty-year-old self. Take control of the game. The whole exercise from meeting her to getting into bed with her takes four stages. The tips I share with you in this book are spread out over these stages. So, let's take a quick look at the stages.

Contact;

This is the process of initiating a conversation or getting her initial attention. Get this stage right, and you are on an express train headed for your goal. This stage is often fraught with doubt and unbridled excitement that can spoil your chances if not reined in. A witty comment, a probing question, or a genuine compliment, there are many ways to open your campaign in a big way.

Attract;

This is perhaps the most decisive stage. So, you now have her attention. That's good, but what do you do with it? She has given you attention, but she is checking you out to see just how attractive you are to her. Handle this stage well, and you will get the majority of her inhibitions off. Get this stage right, and she will be ready to move on to the next level with you.

Flirt;

Okay. So many people believe the first two stages of being the harder stages because they need some form of courage or something, but I think this is the stage that calls for most wit. It is the stage for psychological games and techniques that lay the bed for later. This is the stage where she decides what she wants with you if you allow her to. Alternatively, if you are smart about the way you manipulate the interaction, you can actually get to make suggestions and condition her mind to better favor you. Here, the goal is all about getting close but not too close. Physical contact, suggestive body language, and hanging statements all play a part to help you move her along faster.

Seduce;

If you get to this stage, then all you need do is follow the flow. If she has allowed you get right here, you can be sure she is in the mood too. A lot can change here quickly though, things that are not entirely within your control. The vast majority of the time, though, things are going to go just as well as you hoped for.

The most common mistakes you shouldn't make

Now, what are the most common mistakes men commit that makes them not get laid? We could list dozens together as I am sure you know quite a few of the ones you have been making but let's discuss the most common ones.

Sequencing mistake

Unless she is so actively interested in a good lay that she does not care who she gets it from, you are not going to get laid if you skip any of the four stages above or fail to follow them in order. For instance, if you skip the "Attraction" stage, and jump from the opening to clear flirting, you may just get her turned off. You communicate that you are looking for sex too blandly that way. She isn't going to want to look cheap. So, you had lost before you even started.

Obviously, if your opening sounds too personal, as if you were already in the attraction stage, you communicate a sense of being rude and taking her for granted. Closed doors that is. You can move fast but do not omit any of the stages, and do not put the cart before the donkey. It is guaranteed to backfire spectacularly.

Previous experiences

I definitely had numerous failures before I learned the ropes of the game. Everybody does. I may have more success with the opposite sex, but I still get rejected frequently. That's the whole point of the game; to learn to be accepted more often than you are rejected. The game is not about not being rejected; it never has and will never be. However, I get it that rejection can dampen your spirit but hey, why should it? For every that girl doesn't find you that interesting, I bet that there a dozen within that same block who would jump into your bed if you know your game well enough. So, there is really no point in taking rejection to heart. If she rejects because she is committed to another, then, that is her saving you a whole lot of trouble down the line.

Inexperience

Let's face it. This is the root of all mistakes. Inexperience or the wrong kind of experience can make you lose control of the game. It can force you to chicken out or press harder than is necessary. It can cost you valuable progress or stunt your progress. The only way out of inexperience is to gather more experience by trying out more often.

Inaccurate Stereotyping

"She is so beautiful that I can't have her" has done more harm to more men than outright rejection by ladies. Do not automatically assume she's way out of your league because nobody is. Casanova is famous for having bedded many noblewomen, yet he was not an Adonis or a wealthy noble himself. Do you get my point? The only thing you need to up at any time is your ante. Do not ever underestimate yourself or assume she is taken or too beautiful or way out of your league.

A Lack of confidence

We have talked about confidence before. So, I will just leave you with this message. You are going to be only as successful as you are confident with the women. Women love confident men, and you need to become one. I will explain how later.

Lack of a tried system

Everybody who is good at their work or hobby practiced and developed a working system or set of routines that enabled them to be that good. Routines and habits are planned impulses that act as shortcuts for you. Besides that, having a particular system makes things much easier for you. You know what to do next and what to say. You get to improvise along the way, but having a set routine gives you a firm foundation to build upon.

Well, this chapter was all about introducing you to women and the things you need to win them over. I have also explained some of the more common mistakes you shouldn't be making. Now, the bulk of this book follows. The next chapters all contain key info and techniques that can help you become the player you have always wanted to be. Read on.

CHAPTER TWO

TIP 1; THE MINDSET THAT NEVER FAILS

You can have everything going for you with a girl, but if you are not in the right mindset, you will still not get down with her. To be in the right moment is to be filled with confidence and have a spring in your step. Okay. You may get one or two girls even on an off-day, but unless you are really in the groove and in the right mental state, you will scare off any prospective e girls you are trying to land. What is the right mental state to approach girls for a pickup?

Well, there is no specific mental state as such, but you obviously have a better chance when you are relaxed and looking to catch fun. You are not about to pick up a girl so easily when you are angry or in the grasp of negative emotions such as grief or panic. A more accomplished player can function in almost all scenarios, but if you are still a relative novice, you are not getting any numbers at that funeral.

So, here is what you should do. Why do you want a woman's company at that moment? To have fun, right? By that same logic, you have to hold a promise of fun yourself. Your insides have to be buzzing for you to leave a lasting enough impression that she wants more of you.

Be in the mood, be in the moment. In fact, be the moment. Worry less about the reception you are going to get and focus more on working yourself into the right pitch. Often, what you are going to say to a lady mirrors your internal state. If you are not feeling like fun inside you, the chances are high that you will end up being a bore or getting bored. Work on your mood, be in the moment, and get ready to have fun. If you are not in this mental state, you might as well get ready for a night full of rejection or pick up one of the girls you have been with, in the past. There is going to be a slim chance of a new catch.

CHAPTER THREE

TIP 2; BREAK DOWN YOUR APPROACH INTO SMALL STEPS

So, you think you are in the right mood for some game tonight, and you have hit up the local club to seek out fresh targets or someone to keep you sexual company. You are in the club, and a lot of potential marks are hovering around. You finally zero on one or spot a woman that seems to fit the bill. Here is the first obstacle most novices face.

"Do I walk up to her," "How can I be sure she is even alone" or "I don't think she is going to be interested" kinds of thoughts probably flow through your mind. These cause you to slow down, chip away at your confidence, and lower your odds of engaging her. For a lot of people, the whole process looks way too complex and big for them to pull off. So, mentally, they are already steeling themselves for one harrowing experience. It matters not if they can hold the conversation for long, or it is a short, brief one. They are already technically defeated because they see a mountain in front of them.

To succeed, you have to understand that the whole game is played in stages. Your brief is to start from the first stage and pull her through the stage. Then, you up the ante, move up a gear and watch to see if she is after you. To do this, you need to break the mountain that represents the game. It is a lesson straight from NLP classes for procrastination. You are less likely to do something you consider bulky and complex. So, you need to divide the game into bits and play it one bit after the other. That way, you can focus on just one aspect at a time.

Let's take a Mr. James as a hypothetical example. James is seating at a bar and notice a beautiful lady with two of her friends on the other side of the room. James hasn't had much success with ladies recently, but there was something about this one that caught his attention. Usually, he only got to approach two out of every girl he admired, and he only always got the full attention of one. The odds are stacked against him as usual. As he is thinking over whether he should make an approach, the three ladies stood up, clearly ready to live.

As if on cue, James drags himself off his stool and in their general direction. Good so far, right? Yes. Well, except for the wide smile plastered on his face, our hero James is burning up inside. As he gets close to the ladies, he is yet to decide on his opening statement. He isn't even sure of his plan for getting the attention of the right lady. He clearly also needs to make provisions for her friends and find a way to divest her from their company for a brief period. Of course, he was worried he still carried the stale smell of cigarette smoke from the last stick he had puffed on.

Now, let's hit a pause on our story. Does James look like he is about to make a score or mark yet another rejection? I guess we agree on the correct answer. Why is he about to fail again? It's simply because he has allowed the game to overwhelm him. When you get overwhelmed, you lose the game. That's pretty straightforward. James holds next to no chance of holding that conversation he wants unless the lady herself stops him in his tracks and ask him out, which is not about to happen in a million years.

Do not be like James. The game is in stages, but you also need to make your approach to be in levels. Instead of focusing on everything, tell yourself, "I am going to stop this lady and make a nice comment to get her to talk to me." That sounds so much simpler right. After the opening comment works out all good, you can turn your attention to "I need to find a way to get her to speak to me out of hearing of her friends" or "I need to sound interesting enough for their group."

So long as you have practiced before, moving from stage to stage on impulse is going to be way simpler for you than facing the whole game at once. You don't want to get knocked off or intimidated, which is what happens to a lot of guys.

Instead, focus on breaking down your approach. Divide and conquer these smaller steps, and you will be in the thick of the game before you even realize you are in it at all.

CHAPTER FOUR

TIP 3; KILL THAT LITTLE VOICE WITHIN YOU

Your mind is not a single entity. What you eventually decide to do after thinking is the conclusion that at least two parts of your mind have argued on and reached a conclusion about. Now, when it comes to walking up to a lady and charming her, there are two voices. I call one Paul and the other Peter. Paul is the voice of caution, pessimism, and ego. He is the voice that tells you that you are going to get rejected definitely. He is the voice keeping you on your seat when every other voice wants on your feet spitting lines. Peter, on the other hand, is the voice of unbridled adventure, spurring you on to make fresh attempts. Unfortunately, in most novices, Paul is the stronger voice. Even when you have been able to convince yourself to make an approach, you still continue to hear that little voice within you telling you all the reasons why your mark is going to turn out married.

You know what? You need to keep that little voice shut, especially when you are already in the game. It is often the voice of low esteem and punctures your confidence. The last thing you want is a confidence drain installed right in your mind. So, do not step out there unsure or with your voice in your own head to undermine your efforts. How can you do this?

The smartest way is by making peace with the worst scenario. The worst scenario is to get rejected. I did get slapped once though. When it comes to the game, rejection is pretty standard and does not mean you have not done well enough. It may be due to external factors such as your mark having hostile chaperones around, or perhaps she isn't really interested in anything that leads to sex with you.

It doesn't matter how well your opening line is received; you are still going to need to impress her by going past her initial challenge. You won't get her attention otherwise. Expect that she is going to be a bit laidback and set you one or two challenges at the onset. Do not get fazed if your opener is met with a less-than-favorable reply. Simply ghost your way around that.

Perhaps though, the best way to get rid of the fear is by warming up. In need for a girl for the night? Do not wait until you find the one you want. Do several warm-up attempts. Look at the other lady in the aisle. Walk up to her and compliment her about something. Make sure it is a genuine compliment. Chat with her for a few moments and move on. Try this set on three or four random women before you decide on your actual target. Warming up gets you ready in the groove. It gives you the same benefits athletes get from warming up before the main event. It puts you at ease and helps you shut off that little voice of dissent. It gives you the assurance that you are in control and you can do even better when you actually open your original campaign.

CHAPTER FIVE

TIP 4; MAKING THE RIGHT OPENING

Your opener is going to determine if she pays you attention at all or just walk off. It is also one hard nut for novice to crack. As one of my former students confessed to me, standing in front of an attractive woman, you have designs on, can make you lose half of the vocabulary you have. Well, that is if you are a novice. A true player doesn't experience that, especially when he has acquainted himself with the worst-case scenario.

Your opening statement has to fulfill quite several criteria. You do not want it to sound too boring, or she is going to get out of sight as fast as lightning. Still, you cannot sound too familiar or take too many conveniences for granted. Worst of all, though is to use a common pickup line. This isn't an Austin Powers movie. It is you trying to win yourself a woman for the night. So, do not go all, "Do you know you are beautiful?" or "You have such beautiful eyes." Those mark you out as lazy, uninventive, and lacking originality.

Imagine yourself as a girl and a guy is hitting upon you with the "An angel is missing in heaven, and I think I just found her" line. Does that not make you cringe? Does it not make you want to shut off the person immediately? Well, that is the way the girls you meet feel when you drop common pickup lines that everybody knows.

Let us look at a few rules and techniques that can guide you.

The Five Seconds Rule

You have spotted a girl you like across the room or seated in the park. Do not lose an instant; walk up to her immediately within five seconds. Make that a part of your routine. Do not dally around for too long, or it will seem like you were gathering courage. Women can tell when you have just spent the last few minutes gathering courage to meet them, and they don't like it. It makes them feel weird, which they do not want to. So, apply the five seconds rule. Each time, you come upon a new mark, get the ball rolling within five seconds of meeting her or forget about making that pitch entirely.

Comment or question?

Many people come up to me and ask me which of these two options works better. In my experience, I believe both actually work well if you say the right things, but nothing beats combining the two together. Allow your opening to state a fact or make an observation. That is the comment. Then, follow it up with a poser, a question that involves the opinions of your mark. That pretty much opens things up. Let us look at a sample opener one of my friends used recently here. In his words, "I was at a birthday party recently when I spotted a gorgeous lady. I made my way towards her, and as I drew closer, I noticed her phone cover had one of those little stickers, hers was a picture of Lionel Messi, the Argentine footballer. Instantly, I went,

"Messi is definitely a brilliant player and perhaps the best one on the planet, but I do think not winning anything for his nation is going to count against him in the nearest future surely. On a personal note, though, I prefer the Portuguese, Ronaldo. For me, the difference between them is that of a business lunch and a birthday party like this. I do know I will pick to be in this party talking to someone with such beautiful eyes as yours than be jacked up in a tux".

Now, that may not be the perfect opener of all time, but it does throw the door open for a healthy conversation. He has managed to pique her interest and strike the similar ground in one stroke. She is less likely to resist his next move if she thinks they have a similar hobby or thinks she has a correction to make. In the same opener, too, my friend managed to work

25

in a genuine compliment that is bound to disarm the lady. By being particular, he has told her he likes being with her; that's frank and direct and is always appreciated.

Leave things open

Look at that sample opener again. Can you see how many open spaces he has left to pursue the conversation? Depending on her reply, that conversation could end up anywhere. It could end up being a debate about two footballers or the merits of dressing up in a tux for a business lunch. Leaving such open avenues makes it easier to reply and steer the conversation subtly towards where you want.

Chirp in something about yourself

Too many guys focus on appealing to a lady's sense of chivalry so much that they lose sight of the goal; creating value and worth for themselves. Mention something about yourself. It could be something as basic as your view about something or observation you made. Allow "I" to show up several times at least. That speaks about your value and self-worth.

Be clear you do not intend to take too much time

I know. I know. You are probably wondering what the game is all about if I am asking you to let her perceive that you do not intend to spend too much time. Well, that's a farce. I know you want to spend a lot of time, but making that too clear from the onset is about to slice into the amount of time you actually get in a big way.

Do not open with "Are you busy?', or "Can I join you?". Obviously, that's what you want, but when you put it in words, it gets girls to get their guard up. It also makes you seem available or powerless to resist their charm. Do not sound automatically boring by implying that you want to take a lot of time.

Use humor, not jokes

Do not be the guy that crams jokes and comes to pour them out. She is looking for a man, not a comedian. Instead, introduce light humor. Do not be guilty of overdoing things. Simply make one or two funny comments that fit the scenario unfolding. The worst thing ever is to crack a joke that she cannot relate to. Keep things simple.

I often get asked, "what if I am not funny?" a lot of times. My answer is always the same "Everyone is funny" each time. It's only your mental state that affects your humor. Get relaxed, remain surefooted, calm your mind, be yourself, and the humor will follow through. You cannot be funny when you are all jumped up, or your stomach is in knots. Employ humor

Don't appear too needy or serious

You aren't interviewing somebody for the vacant secretarial role in your office. This is a real human being you are walking up to. Let us not pretend. If you walk up to me, it will cross my mind that you may only be after the goodies. The worst thing to do as a man then, is to appear all too needy or serious about life.

In your opening and the initial phases of contact, do not make an impression of being too demanding or she will poof… into thin air. Keep things simple, sweet, and general at first. The initial opening is meant to open the set and not to win the game.

CHAPTER SIX

TIP 5; CARRY A WINGMAN

If you started playing the game early on, perhaps in high school, you would know the importance of having backup when necessary. Your wingman can help you out in any number of ways. A few years ago, when I first took in my first group of students, I had them pair up for practice and go out into the field to practice. They all reported that they felt calmer when they knew they had a minder looking after them. It didn't even matter that in some cases, they were more experienced at the game than the wingman.

Your wingman gives you variety under different circumstances. He can save you a whole lot of stress when your mark is in a group. Isolating the one lady from a group can be quite cumbersome. This is because of ladies in a group bond together and sticks up for one another. That means you need to first slip past the sensors of the others in the group before you stand a chance at all. Your wingman can help you with that. He can take center-stage and keep the conversation going while you get down to the business of the hour.

Ever been in a tight or rough spot before? Perhaps your conversation is dying off. A great wingman can save you by popping up at the right time to switch topics on cue. Wingmen can also serve to raise your value within a group conversation. Attempting to increase the other person's worth within the group by praising his attitude and personality instantly gives you too further appeal as a great guy who sticks up his friends. Everyone wants a friend or a man like that. That is further validation of social reputation. If you are on the receiving end of the praise even, your reputation still gets a shot in the arm.

CHAPTER SEVEN

TIP 6; PRACTICE YOUR ROUTINE

Practice infront of the mirror!

I don't even need to tell you this, but hey, you need to practice anything to get better at it, right? Flirting and picking up girls is no exception. We all try to be spontaneous, but the truth is that every good player has their routine. Good players smell out targets, approach, entangle and move for the kill in a smooth, practiced routine. It helps to have a rough draft that you follow each time. You can adjust it as circumstances may change, but a general routine helps you work on semi-automation. It also reduces anxiety as you already have contingencies for each response.

Practice your lines in front of a mirror. Work on any speech deficiencies you may have in private. A stutter can kill your punchline if it occurs at the wrong time. Try out your routine on new girls, note its effects and shortcomings; work on it to refine it even better. Every good player of the game has his own custom routine. So, you need one too, and you need to practice it as much as possible.

CHAPTER EIGHT

TIP 7; EVADE THE HOOP; DO NOT TAKE HER TEST

Every lady you meet is going to try this pretty early in your interaction. I call it the personality test. One can only pity the ladies. They get hit upon so many times that it makes absolute sense for them to have a filter in place for any new guy they meet. This comes in the form of challenges. She tries to shake your cool using words or actions and watches out for your reaction.

Most people know this already; what most guys fail to realize, though, is that you do not need to pass the challenge to pass her test. In fact, the moment you try the test, you have failed. The test isn't meant for you to pass. It is only her own way of making the jump through the hoop. Once you do, the game loses the fun for her. It means she can get you to do anything she wants. So, nine times out of ten, when you pass the test, your chance to bed her passes away as well.

Instead, refuse to take the test. In fact, snub the test as if it is not even there. Assert your value by asking her to take it for what you have said it is. For instance, you may be talking about music, and then, she says, "Sing for me. I want to hear your voice". Whatever else you do at that point is all good except singing. She has thrown you a hoop and is watching you closely to see if you jump through it. So, avoid the hoop. You can say, "well, the audience around sure doesn't appreciate an orchestra." Better still, ignore that remark and go on with your conversation.

Or perhaps you mentioned that you write poetry and she goes "Write me a poem. I am sure your poems are sad really", in half-a-joke. Do not get riled up enough to argue with her. She is trying to rattle your confidence and coolness. You can respond to that with something humorous like, "How did you know? I wrote the one that Macbeth read last before he died". She would probably burst out laughing. Test passed without being taken! The moment you write her that poem there or bring out one of your old ones to show her you are good; you have lost the game.

34

Sometimes, a girl is going to throw a bitchy or outright mean remark at you. You may walk up to her and lay your opening out thick and perfect, but only get a "Yes. So, what should I do with that?" You are being tested, and you must not take the test of trying to prove who you are. Instead, you can use either blast through her meanness or ignore it entirely.

You can blast her defense by letting her know you understand why she needs to be hostile to random guys. That also tells her that you are not a random guy that she can throw in the bin. Alternatively, you can just carry on in the previous tones without seeming to take notice of what she has just said. That tells her that you are unaffected at all.

CHAPTER NINE

TIP 8; DEALING WITH "I HAVE A BOYFRIEND."

For most intending players, this is the one great obstacle that they cannot scale. So, when a lady utters those words, it means "Game over" most of the times. News flash; it doesn't have to be. So, you dropped into the bar one day, and you approached a girl you got attracted to. You started a conversation, and things were moving smoothly until she dropped a bombshell, "I think I should tell you I have a boyfriend." So, of course, you automatically drop your interest. Well, that's wrong. Let us look at why.

Every girl has what I like to call the Anti-Slut Defense system. It doesn't matter if she can barely stop herself from tearing your clothes off right there, her defense system is going to hold strong. This ASD system is her own personal guard against being seen as *cheap*. So, you are going to have sweat it out to earn her. Now, when a lady tells you she is in a relationship, it could mean a lot of things.

It could be;

- "Yes, I am in a relationship, but that doesn't stop us from happening."
- She is not in a relationship, but she wants to see the way you respond to that challenge
- She is in a relationship, and she isn't truly interested in a fling with you
- She isn't in a relationship, but she feels she needs to get rid of you.

What can you do when you are presented with this challenge? Do not give up entirely unless she does communicate that she is really, really interested. Okay, I am not without conscience or asking you to bed other people's partners but hey, if she is willing, why shouldn't you be? How do you know if her declaration is genuine and represents a refusal of your approach or is an attempt to play hard?

The only solution is peppering your discussion with a lot of active disinterest and observing her responses to seeding (I will explain how this works later). Do not allow that to serve as a deterrent for you until you are sure it's a major obstacle.

Take particular note if she repeats the same statement with alarming frequency and all seriousness. That may just be a no-go area.

CHAPTER TEN

TIP 9; DON'T PLAY THE AGE OR WEIGHT GAME

Whatever you do, do not play the age or weight game. There is no prize for winning it, but there is a price to be paid for every guess, right or wrong. When conversations get boring, people start to get back to the basics of knowing the people around them. Workplace, hobbies, and interests can serve as topics (Not all the time, though) to pass the time until fresh inspiration comes. Or at least, that's what most people think.

Casting around for basic knowledge is pretty high on my

"No" list. If you must, though, stay away from the age game. Do not get yourself in a corner where you get to tell a potential mark that they are slightly overweight. Or worse, try to guess their age or search for potential markers for their age. You are bound to lose.

If you underestimate her age, you have alienated her, and that conversation will not leave that table. If you overestimate her age, you are telling her that she has aged more than is normal. No lady likes that. Do not play the age game; do not play the weight game. Any other game but those two would be better.

CHAPTER ELEVEN

TIP 10; DO NOT SELF-DEPRECATE OR SCORE CHEAP POINTS

It is the master comedian's ultimate last resort. When you cannot find anything funny to talk about, turn against yourself, and make fun of yourself. That's always funny.

STOP right there. The idea above is valid everywhere except when you are in front of a girl or woman you want. You do need all the value you can get in front of her and spewing out your weaknesses is surely not adding any value to you whatsoever.

If you are in a group, do not make a habit of poking fun at others in the group either. That communicates a lack of class. It may earn you a few laughs, but laughter isn't your end goal, is it?

CHAPTER TWELVE

TIP 11; THE PEACOCK TECHNIQUE; MAKE PASSIVE CONFIRMATION OF CREDIBILITY WORK FOR YOU

The best way to make yourself the center of attraction in a room is by actually creating enough attention to hold everyone's focus if only for a few moments. This is known as the peacock technique. Have you ever seen a peacock and not look twice? I guess not.

By its colorful plumage, a peacock calls attention to itself at every moment of the day. When it spreads it's tail feathers wide, everyone around is conscripted to take a glance or two or stare at how beautiful the scene is. You can garner this same attention differently too.

N.B; This is no technique for the newbie, as it entails a supreme level of confidence.

I mentioned social confirmation and credibility in the first chapter. Well, one way of using it to your advantage is by revealing bits about yourself *almost accidentally.* The next best way is actually to get it all up and flaunt it subtly. At a party, the most outlandish-dressed female always gets a lot of attention, all other things being equal. This is because everyone is subconsciously drawn to her. Everyone wants to understand the woman behind the outlandish dress for either noble or *un-noble* reasons. Whatever your intentions, though, you are already at a psychological disadvantage when you walk up to her; she knows she has all the attention and upgrades her demeanor automatically to match this.

Well, even men can apply the peacock technique. How? Good (or expensive) dressing always says "Hey there," even before your mouth has opened. Dressing to kill has always held intrigue for women. Firstly, it confirms that you are in the know-how, a man who understands the groove and dresses to match that as well. Secondly, it reflects your taste. It means when you approach her; you think she is of high class too. That helps you thaw the initial freeze just a little bit. But in this game, we take all the help we can get.

The peacock technique isn't about the dressing alone, though. You can apply it in a variety of ways. You can leverage your finances, fame, or even academic prowess depending on the company you are trying to pick up. If you have it, you can flaunt it on the low.

There is a caveat to this technique, though. It is only half-guaranteed to succeed as it also relies heavily on the perception that the technique creates in the woman opposite you. Your chances are much better when you combine it with passive disinterest. This is because there is a risk of overdoing things, appearing super-arrogant or fake.

I had a little, *dishonest* technique I used back in college. It goes this way. I was valedictorian at high school, and I attended the same college as my best friend, Jerry. Many times, we often served as each other's wingman. Now, each time he was mine, he had a little routine we had developed. I would walk up to a girl and engage her. A few minutes later, Jerry would burst into the room, stroll about, and *suddenly* spot me. He would then bound over to shake my hands and pump them vigorously like a long-lost friend. I would reply enthusiastically too. Somewhere along the lines, I would mention something like; "Hey Jerry, still bat as fast as ever?" That was his cue for "Yeah. But not as fast as the smartest brain in the whole of XXX school. Still got them brains here?"

We would chat a bit about random things; he would get introduced and soon be in his way. Well, what do you think that little detour always caused? More interest all the time, every time. It was always an ice-breaker, and that little chat always threw up a vista of things I could discuss right after with the girl. Somewhere in the back of her head, she always knew "this is a smart one at least."

You can work out a routine along this line too. Work in an offhand comment that shows your credibility. It may not be enough to get you laid on its own, but it gives you a firmer base to build upon and brightens your chances better. Remember, it is key to validate your social credibility in an abstruse, almost off-hand manner that doesn't make it seem like a big deal.

CHAPTER THIRTEEN

TIP 12; MAKE ACTIVE DISINTEREST A WEAPON OF CHOICE

By far, this is the most important technique you will learn in this book. If it's the only thing you master, then you are already on the way to becoming a master player of the game. Let's hit the pause button a bit and get down to what this is all about.

Let me borrow Neil Strauss's words to explain the concept. "The trick when you're flirting is figuring how to keep a balance between being engaging enough to retain a woman's attention and not seeming overly available."

In a way, the art of seduction needs you to take two steps forward to arouse suspicion and interest, then take a step back to leave your target in confusion. By teasing her like that, you get to raise her interest in your next move while subtly creeping closer to her each time. The best part is that it is not even elaborate or complex. By dropping the right hints in your statement, you can supercharge her interest in you.

Saying the right thing all night will only get you, "Good night. You were good company" kind of farewell. It isn't going to get you even a sensual kiss not to talk of getting her on your bed. It's the good guys who get to be boring. The real players are bad guys. Haven't heard the saying, "Girls love bad guys?"

Why do love stories sell so well in movies? Well, each love story has many emotional ups and downs. That is what makes it a good love story. A love story cannot be on the up all the time, or it will lose its flavor and appeal. In fact, it is the downs that make the ups so sweet. The basic idea of active disinterest is to simulate these ups and downs.

One moment, you sound all nice and romantic. The next moment, you have dropped a corny, or mean the line that gets her mildly annoyed, intrigued, or challenged. For instance, in the middle of your conversation, you go,

"You know, if only you had more hair, I could have dated you." Or she pulls your ear and you go, "Mission aborted. She is too wild and violent for me".

Harmless statements, right? You better believe not. In the first stamen, by playfully admitting that she was a target of a romantic approach, you have piqued her interest. But before she can react to such an approach, you have also implied that she has been ruled out. That is a new situation for a girl. She is used to ruling people out and not being ruled out by men herself. By ruling her out, you have reordered the whole game and turned things upside down. The onus and challenge now for her is to get back on top of the game.

Remember the hoop I told you to avoid, you only just set one of yours. Since girls aren't used to evading and dealing with these hoops, the chances are high that she will jump one of yours. It is good is he attempts the jump but even better if she makes the game of playing the active disinterest game too.

If she goes, "well, thank God we aren't going to date," she has fallen into a trap. It means she thought you were going to have something in common, which gives you a nice angle to flip the whole story around and say, "Oh, so you were planning on dating me. Well, don't lose hope just yet". This line of conversation alone can give you as much time as you want to stoke the sexual tension between the two of you further.

You cannot get into bed with a lady if there is no sexual tension between the two of you. The best way to generate this is by feigning pointed disinterest. Kindly note that there is a thin line between feigned meanness and outright boorishness or insults. Do not ever attempt to cross this line; be mindful of it always. You will get the chance to do as you like later on as soon as you keep your cool.

There is no effective flirting without passive disinterest worked into it. It is the surest, shortest way to create sexual tension that can lead you down *that* path you seek.

CHAPTER FOURTEEN

TIP 13; THE ONLY THING WOMEN CANNOT RESIST

Woman want many different things at the same time. Half of your successful attempts to hold a conversation or build bridges were just as close to failure. There is one universal thing women cannot get enough of, though; sincere, genuine compliments.

Compliments make everyone feel good and great with themselves when it comes down to it, and women are no exceptions. In fact, women ride the crest of compliments more than men. Virtually every guy out there knows this already. So, why do so many guys fail at generating the appropriate response to the compliments they have paid?

The reason is that most compliments are either too insincere or common. Take "You are very beautiful" for instance. How many times do you think a genuinely beautiful girl gets that line on average in a day? Or a week? That means you are repeating what everyone tells her. A beautiful girl already knows she is beautiful and pretty. She doesn't need you to tell her that. Also, that line sounds rather automated, like you had kept it well in advance. "You look pretty" sounds like something you go around saying to every girl you meet.

Instead of offering generic and shallow compliments, take time out to do it the right way. Your compliment does not need to be sincere, but it sure needs to sound so. You need to strike out to offer a compliment that is so specific that it is unique. To do this, I often advise that you make non-physical compliments. They often sound truer and more specific. If you must compliment a lady's physical appearance, then you need to make your compliment to be about a specific part.

Consider the lines below;

"Ladies with oval faces are almost always beautiful. You are surely further proof of that theory".

"I do like the way your mouth turns up when you smile. I think it's very beautiful."

How do they sound to you? Do they look what the other guy might have just said to her now? I bet not. You need to compliment with a reason, and if it is physical, it has to be about a specific point and sound sincere enough.

What I meant above about nonphysical compliments may include touching on something such as how good she's at fashion or whatever she does for a living. It could be about how well-read, fashionable, or quick-witted she is. Take these examples below;

"It is rare to find a lady who understands and treasure Sherlock Holmes stories as much as you do. I find it refreshing to be able to talk about the characters and stories with you".

"I like your fashion style. Simple, trendy and smart but it sure does get the knockers off half the men in every room you enter".

There is no doubt that the lady in question feels like the compliment is actually meant for her. All the examples are personalized to ensure that she gets the message. That singular fact makes it appear as if you were saying the truth, regardless of whether you are or not. Always aim to make your lines different and customized to suit your conditions.

CHAPTER FIFTEEN

TIP 14; DECIPHERING AND UTILIZING BODY LANGUAGE AND PHYSICAL CONTACT

Body language is an important indicator of your progress with your target lady. In the first place, your own body language must support your game. A body language that says you her nervous or not confident will rub off in a wrong way to make the atmosphere awkward. When situations get awkward, your marks develop very fast legs to zoom out of the situation.

Physical contact is another important tool for you. Almost imperceptibly, work in slight physical touches to charge up the conversation. Do not be intrusive. A light pat on the back of her hand, a little nudge on the shoulder, a light smack on the arm, work in these little touches that validate your assertiveness and control over the flow of the conversation. Keep the heavier touches and slightly more sensitive parts out of the game for much later. The touches and her body language also help serve to tell you how comfortable she is getting with you.

If for instance, you lean in with your head and say something to her, and she automatically jerks her head out of range. That's a sure "Whoa Mr. Man. Not that fast!" Slow down and get another attempt. It means you need to work on getting more value and credibility before you make your move.

After you have employed full-on flirting, and you are ready to move onto something more hands-on, you need to assess her "interest" indicators. By studying certain signs that expose just how comfortable a lady is getting with you, you can easily determine if the time is right to make your first move at getting things to the next level.

How comfortable is she with talking to you? Does she pull back when you make physical contact? Does she rise up to your hoops and play the flirting game with you? How does she respond to the silences in conversation? Does she try to resume the conversation and broach new topics? Any hint or actual suggestive facial expressions? Has she said anything contrary to the night ending up somewhere desirable to you? Does she glance at her watch frequently or seem lost in time? Have you laid the groundwork for the next phase?

There is no fireproof way of detecting if she is ready for proper seduction than to make a move. Her response is the only thing that will tell you if you have built up enough value to get her clothes off. Next tip deals with that.

CHAPTER SIXTEEN

TIP 15; SEED, SEED, AND SEED

What do you do if you want to harvest oranges next year? Plant a seed in time, right? Well, the same thing applies to women. If you want to end up in bed with a lady you just met, then you need to plant the idea somewhere in her mind early enough and leave it to germinate. Seeding is the technique of making coded suggestions that you then return to act upon.

You cannot just pop up and ask, "can we have sex?" in whatever format you choose if you have not laid the groundwork properly. The suggestion needs to be there in such a way that as the night or day draws to a close, it becomes obvious where you are headed to. You need to use active disinterest to reignite her consciousness and touch the seed you planted every once in a while.

As the day or night draws to a close, if you have played the game well and you have had enough fun dancing, partying or throwing sexual innuendoes at each other, the interest indicators should be flashing green loudly for you to make the final move. How you choose to play that then depends on what you want? A future date or a no-holds, no attachment night of sex.

Let's assume you want another date perhaps because you think this may go further than just sex or because you are not sure she is in for a one-night stand that particular day. Getting her to drop her contact details should be easy enough if you have pressed the right buttons. For clarity sake and because some guys find it hard to execute this part, let me drop a few pointers for you.

Do not ask for her phone number without an obvious reason. Do not ask for her number then try to set up a date. Instead, make a date first. You need to seed the date sometime before you ask. If I meet a lady who is in town for a few weeks but loves the arts, I may casually mention that such-and-such museum in town really has some nice pieces she should see. I don't need to invite her to go see the pieces with me in the first place. As the evening draws to a close, I may then ask her, "Hey, you know what. Are you free next week on Thursday? I can go show you some of the pieces I mentioned."

Obviously, that invitation wasn't meant for just sightseeing. It is loaded with messages. It is basically, "Can I get a second date?" I have given her room for plausible deniability. She can accept without feeling *cheap*. I have catered to her ego and her desire to see me again, at the same time. It is much more likely that she will accept that date than if I had said: "Can we see each other next week?" The latter question implies that I am taking responsibility or asking. It leaves her no room to maneuver, and women do love to maneuver.

The same rule applies to get her home for some good sex the same night. If a woman wants you, she still might not come out to tell you. It is up to you to move the frame of the game from whatever public place you are, to somewhere more secluded and private obviously.

To do this, you need to seed her early in the game. Seed a reason why she should go see your home in her mind. Any harmless reason would do. I have tried various versions of "I have a great playlist you should listen to" "Do you want to see the paintings I have," "you should taste my venison soup" and "The décor I just got for my home really amazes first-time visitors."

Work lines like that into your conversation early on and leaves it at that. When it is time to hit the home-base, you only need to throw an offer to go show her that interesting thing at home. Mostly, if she is already into you, any excuse at all will do. She just needs an excuse to get up, move with you, and allow things escalate rapidly.

Naturally, when you activate the seed you have planted in her mind, you will get one of three responses.

-Yes, I will like to see XXX that you have

-Yes, I will like to see XXX but not tonight. I have to be up early tomorrow etc.

-I am not really that interested in XXX. Thank you but no sweat.

The last statement is the dreaded plateau. It means you have lucked out and you are not getting laid, not that night anyway. The first statement is an express visa. If you get to that point, you can mentally close this book and let things flow naturally.

The second statement is a little bit dicey. That statement could be a polite but determined refusal of your sexual advance. It could be "Thanks, but I do not want to go beyond flirting with you." It could also be a genuine "I will like to have sex with you, but I genuinely have to be up early tomorrow. So, no chance of a hangover". How should you deal with that?

An experienced player knows when the game is slipping out or when it is a genuine excuse. You should probably follow your gut. Whatever the case, if the statement is firm enough, there is a huge chance that you will actually not be getting down with that particular lady that particular night. There is a window of hope, though. So, just play it cool and either (1) Beat a retreat and wait for *when* she is available or (2) Try to build up even more value and then make a fresh attempt. The chances do not favor the second option, but if you are just insistent enough without becoming annoying, you just may get lucky.

CHAPTER SEVENTEEN

TIP 16; MOVING IN FOR THE KILL

This is the last tip I offer you. Why? If you get here, you will probably coast to home base. I don't have to teach you how to handle home-base, right?

In moving in for the kill, the kiss is always the starting point. If you get that long, sensual, French -kiss, you can be sure you are home and true on point.

The location of the first kiss matters a lot too. I have had first kisses right there where I made the opening. I have had first kisses after the second club that night. I have had first kisses a week later, and I have first kisses thirty minutes after my first words.

If you are an absolute newbie and you have gotten her to agree to go home *to check something,* you may want to hold off until you get home. Why? I don't want your confidence getting shattered by a fitting slap or scorn if you have misinterpreted her indicators. If you have gotten her home, on the other hand, it is safe to assume that she is into you already and somewhere in her mind, she has mentally prepared for your attempt.

Sometimes, the sexual tension is so strong that she may literally grab your lips right in the car or cab on your way home, or immediately after you set your foot in the house. That simplifies your work. If she doesn't though, perhaps because she is shy or so bold that she wants you to make a move first, here is how to go about things.

Get her comfortable with your home to dispel all shyness. Put on some music, and get her a light drink. A common trick is the salad technique. Prepare to cut up fruits and offer some to her. Do not make the mistake of cutting up fruits then though. Instead, cut them up before you go out on a search for a girl. Those few moments you spend ravaging your kitchen *and cutting up fruits* mean that she has a few moments to adjust and gives her the feeling that you are not rushing her.

Most importantly, eating a salad together gives you a perfectly legitimate excuse to get close to her and reinitiate

63

contact. Remember that this technique is only for super-shy girls. If she isn't super-shy, I suggest you get down to business quick.

You can also try to spice up the atmosphere a little bit by having some great music playing at a low volume. This is extra though. If she is still in your house at this time, you are likely going to get something done.

How do you communicate the intention of the first kiss? There are two common techniques I want to discuss here. The first one is the **stare down technique.**

Here, eye contact is the key. Allow a few moments to pass in silence. Kill all chances of a conversation by making noncommittal sounds when she tries to talk. The silence is going to get a bit disconcerting. Look into her eyes and away quickly when she looks at you. Do that once or twice. Then, hold her gaze for longer. Flutter your eyelids a little bit. Lean your head towards her and go for the kiss. This is one technique that seems never to fail. It is the most widely used technique among great players as it rarely fails. If it fails, chances are you were never in with a shot of getting a kiss.

A second, bolder approach is **the direct teasing method**. After you must have caused some silence to be observed, hold her gaze, and lick your lips. Ask her what she was looking at. Something like "Don't even tell me you were looking at my lips. They are off-limits. Or maybe, they are not." Allow the laughter that follows to die into silence. Hold her gaze and ask boldly; "Do you want to kiss me?". Do not wait for an answer. Lean in and take your kiss. What comes after is solely yours to decide.

If you have followed all the steps correctly, and you get to pick off that kiss, you can be reasonably assured that you have succeeded in seducing her. I am not teaching you how to have great sex. My remit was to get you sex. Now, do a good job of it and get some success off my tips.

CONCLUSION

If you have followed my advice up to the last chapter, then congratulations. I believe you are going to have a better deal of trying to get the girls that tickle your fancy. It matters not who they are; the game is all yours to play. The key is in understanding the principles that move women.

They do not want the things (or men) that others may not want. They want the men other women want. They want the man who is not fazed by them. They want a sure, confident man who knows his worth and does not pander to their every need. They want a bad boy. It is the allure. They want a manly man, who knows what he wants and does not buckle under the emotional pressure of standing and conversing with a strange, beautiful woman. Throw in humor, fun, a great physical appearance, and natural talent, and you have yourself a winning hand at all times.

Luckily, I hope I have been able to show you that every man has a bit of all these. In any case, unless you are planning for the long-term, no one is going to ask you to demonstrate proof of who you are. The goal, in fact, is in remaining a mystery. There is no seduction or flirting without mystery and light, unpleasant surprises. It is the only way of building up the sexual tension that she feels she needs the sex to get back to earth.

Yes, you know what you want, she knows what you want, but you need to make her question what you want for the game to be worthwhile. A plain approach holds no promises or surprises. It makes you look bland and predictable. It turns women off and defeats you.

Buildup value, engage her attention, be a great flirt, employ active disinterest to brutal efficiency and remain composed all through, and that initial "Hi" can turn to something more erotic, banal and carnal in no time at all.

It is the most engaging game there is on the planet, and you need to learn to be a good player to join the winning team. Good luck!!!

Printed in Great Britain
by Amazon